FRAN HODGKINS

THE SECRET
GALAXY

Photographs by Mike Taylor

TILBURY HOUSE PUBLISHERS, THOMASTON, MAINE

Seeing Stars

The light from homes, offices, stores, vehicles, and street lamps can make stars hard to see at night. This is called light pollution.

Seeing stars is easier where (or when) there are fewer lights. If you go stargazing, give your eyes a few minutes to get used to the dark.

Put together from many separate night-time satellite photos, this image shows permanent lights on Earth's surface. The most urbanized areas glow the brightest, while areas such as deep jungle, tundra, and desert show few lights.

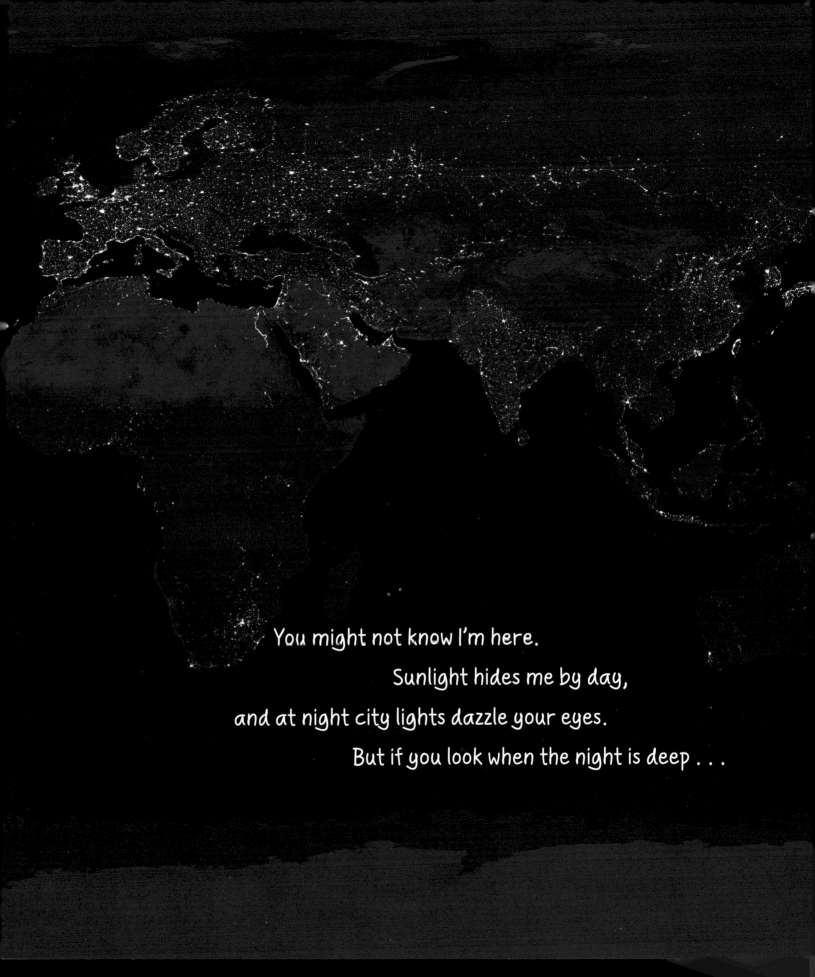

You might not know I'm here.

Sunlight hides me by day,

and at night city lights dazzle your eyes.

But if you look when the night is deep . . .

. . . you'll see me stretched across the sky
from horizon to horizon.
The ancient Greeks named me the Milky Way,
because to them I looked like
milk spilled in the night sky.
Their word for "milk" became
the word galaxy.
I am the Milky Way galaxy.

The Milky Way

The Milky Way galaxy is a spinning disk of gas, dust, and billions of stars, including our sun. When we look across the plane of our vast galaxy, we see the glowing ribbon of stars we call the Milky Way, as in this photo. But all the stars we can see distinctly in the night sky—within the milky ribbon and outside it—are in our galaxy. Some of these make up constellations such as Orion and the Big Bear, and many of them have planets. Using powerful telescopes, we've discovered thousands of *exoplanets* (planets outside our solar system) in the Milky Way so far, and many more remain to be discovered.

In places without light pollution, the Milky Way can be the most noticeable feature in the night sky. It looks like a wide ribbon of stars.

Moving Fast While Sitting Still

Think you're sitting still while reading? Guess again. In the time it takes to read this sentence, you have moved nearly two miles (3.2 km) due to Earth's rotation alone. And at the same time, Earth is going around the sun at nearly 67,000 miles per hour and our solar system is moving around the galaxy's center at 450,000 miles every hour. If you could run that fast, you could go from New York to Los Angeles in about 20 seconds!

Dizzy yet?

Even though the Milky Way galaxy is spinning so fast, it takes about 230 million years to complete a rotation. One revolution ago, dinosaurs were just beginning to roam Earth.

This artist's rendering shows what the Milky Way galaxy would look like if we could see it from above the disk.

I whirl in a spiral with my starry arms trailing.
You and Earth and your sun and solar system
are on one arm, but don't worry.
Gravity holds everything together.
You won't get left behind.

Sun

A Lot of Zeroes!

One hundred billion is a 1 followed by 11 zeroes. How big a number is that? Just one billion grains of sand would fill a dump truck. You would need 100 trucks to hold a hundred billion grains of sand, and 2,000 trucks to hold 2 trillion grains, one for every galaxy in the universe.

I contain more than 100 billion stars—
maybe four times that many—and your sun is just one of them.
And there are at least 2 trillion other galaxies like me in the visible universe.
Your ancestors have watched me from the dawn of history,
but I don't give up my secrets easily.

As Earth rotates, the Milky Way
seems to rise in the east and move
westward across the sky.

Not everyone thought of milk when they looked at me.

In China I was called the Silver River.

Scandinavians called me Vintergaten, their word for winter road;

and the Thai used the name

"Path of the White Elephant."

Time Traveling With Just a Look

When you look up into the sky, you're really looking back in time. You aren't seeing the stars as they are, but as they used to be. Light moves incredibly fast—more than 670,000,000 miles an hour. If you could move that fast, in just one second you could circle the earth seven and a half times! But even at that speed, light from other stars takes a very long time to reach us.

On the picture of the Milky Way shown earlier, you wouldn't be able to tell the sun from Proxima Centauri, the star closest to us. However, light from that star travels more than four years before it reaches Earth. That's how far away the stars are.

Nothing is really as it seems in this photo, because the stars may actually have changed since the light that we see left them. Some of them may no longer be shining at all.

The Algonquin viewed me as the path of departed warriors,

and the Micmac said I was made of firebirds.

To the Cherokee I was corn meal scattered by a naughty dog.

Bad dog!

Secrets of the Aurora

If you live in northern lands, you may see the Milky Way behind the aurora borealis, or northern lights. These spectral shrouds of light form in the upper regions of Earth's atmosphere when particles from the sun interact with Earth's magnetic field. Expanding, contracting, red or green, ghostly or intense, northern lights are an awe-inspiring sight. The Inuit people said the lights were a result of a ball game between people or perhaps between walruses.

. . . .

Northern lights glow brightly against a backdrop of stars in this photo taken at Pemaquid Point, Maine.

Time Passages

For much of human history, Earth was believed to be the center of the universe, with the sun, planets, and stars in orbit around it. Some early scientists who challenged this belief suffered for their ideas, sentenced to prison or even death. Today's astronomers stand on the shoulders of pioneering scientists as they learn more about the universe.

What am I really?

I am neither milk nor corn meal, nor birds nor roads,

though you could say that I've given birth to all those things.

I am made of dust, gas, stars, and planets.

The wonders of Earth and the sky come together in this photo of the Milky Way and the Corona Arch, located just outside Moab, Utah. Although millions of years old, Corona Arch is much younger than the galaxy.

Stars are born in giant clouds of gas and dust.

The most massive of them burn fast and die after a few hundred thousand years, but small stars can live billions of years—maybe longer.

B

Since the universe began,
nearly 14 billion years have passed.
I've been around for more
than 13 billion of those years.
I've seen stars born, live, and die.

A

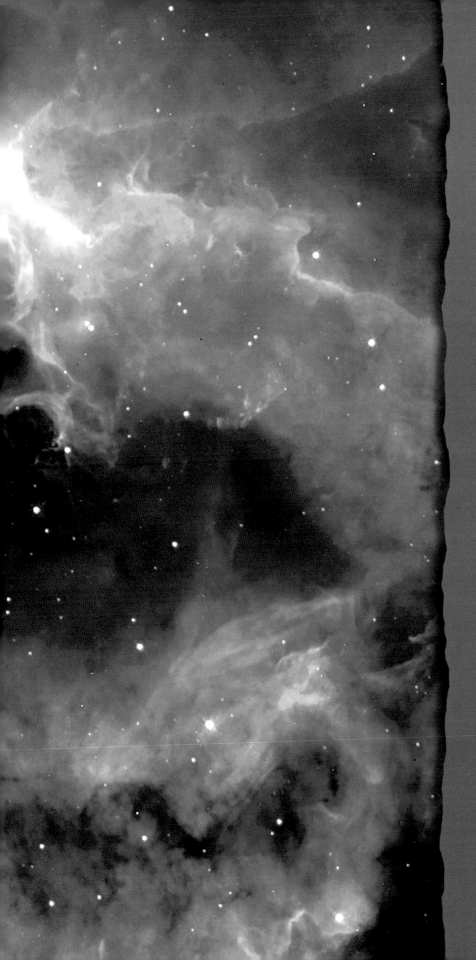

A Starry Nursery

If conditions are right, dust and gas collapse and condense to form a star. New stars are born in great clouds of gas and dust called nebulas.

Stars glow in different colors because they are different temperatures. The hottest, most intense stars glow blue. Moderately hot stars like our sun are yellow. Old, cooler stars are usually red.

There is a lot of dust in the galaxy—so much dust, in fact, that we can't see everything even with our most powerful optical telescopes. Scientists use other wavelengths of electromagnetic radiation—such as radio waves and infrared—to see. Unlike visible light, those wavelengths pass easily through cosmic shrouds of dust.

Stars are near birth and near death in this image of a giant nebula. Newborn stars will soon emerge from the bright pillar of gas and dust at A. The bright blue star at B will soon explode into a supernova.

It's Elementary

Carbon, oxygen, and nitrogen are three elements that are essential to life on Earth. Without them, life as we know it—including this ancient tree in the desert and you—would not exist. As the astronomer Carl Sagan said, "We are star-stuff."

This tree is in Dead Horse Canyon State Park in Utah.

Earth and all the planets are made of the stuff of stars,
and every living thing contains atoms born in stars.
From the calcium in your bones to the iron in your blood, nearly
everything in you was forged inside a star long ago.

The Death of a Star

Stars like the sun glow because deep within their cores, atoms are being fused together into new, larger atoms. Hydrogen atoms become helium atoms. This fusion releases a huge amount of energy that can take tens of thousands of years to reach a star's surface. But once that energy reaches the surface of our sun, it takes only eight minutes to reach Earth as light.

Fusion goes on until all of a star's hydrogen has been fused into helium. What happens next depends on the star's mass—the amount of matter it contains.

The Butterfly Nebula formed when a star ran out of fuel and ejected its outer layers. Many of the star's atoms are now flying through space. The dying star's core remains, hidden between the "wings."

Within each star, atoms fuse,
building element after element.
When fusion stops,
a small or medium star (like your sun) ejects its outer
layers into space, possibly to be recycled
into new stars and planets.

Without the outward pressure created by fusion,
gravity takes over and the star's core collapses.
The force is so great that atoms first
touch and then crunch into each other.
The star shrinks to a white dwarf.
Bigger stars meet an even more violent end.
The biggest become black holes.

Space rocks, or meteoroids, wander through our
solar system, some as small as sand grains, some
as large as small asteroids. When one enters Earth's
atmosphere at high speed, it becomes a fireball
blazing across the sky. These are meteors, but since
ancient times we've called them shooting stars.

A Massive Star's Fate

A massive star meets a violent end. Instead of puffing its outer layers into space like a small or medium star, it experiences a huge explosion called a supernova. Its atoms are thrown outward across space—all but the core. It collapses into a neutron star, or, if the star is very massive, becomes a black hole.

Seeing Indirectly

Although they can't be seen directly, black holes give themselves away. A black hole will affect the movement of objects nearby. It may make gas and dust around it move very quickly and give off X-rays and other forms of radiation that betray the black hole's presence.

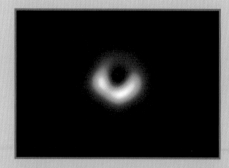

The first-ever image of a black hole, obtained in 2019, shows a bright ring of light bent by the intense gravity around the black hole at the center of Galaxy M87. This black hole is 6.5 billion times more massive than our sun.

In this artist's conception, a black hole's powerful gravity tears away gas from a nearby star.

Light can't escape from a black hole,
and matter doesn't stand a chance.
Black holes suck up gas, dust, and stars—anything that comes too close.
What happens inside a black hole?
That's another secret.

At the Heart of the Galaxy

The black hole at the center of the Milky Way is called Sagittarius A-star (or SgrA* for short). Supermassive black holes may be at the center of every galaxy. These black holes are far more massive than the sun, but pack that mass into a very small space. As a result, supermassive black holes have unbelievably strong gravity. They pull in the stars and gas near the center of the galaxy, growing even more massive as they do.

The Milky Way's black hole is pretty calm, but it's a different story for some other galaxies. In 2020, astronomers using X-ray and radio telescope data found evidence of the biggest explosion yet seen in the universe. The eruption from a supermassive black hole at the center of a galaxy 390 million light years from Earth punched a hole in surrounding hot cosmic gases big enough to swallow fifteen Milky Way galaxies!

An artist created this image based on what scientists know about supermassive black holes. At the edge of the black hole, a place called the event horizon, time and reality may be quite different from what we know.

A black hole lives at my heart, too,
but it's different from one formed by a star.
My black hole has the mass of four million suns,
yet it could fit inside Earth's orbit around the sun.

I'm not only stars and planets,

but also the mysterious, guessed-at stuff in between that

makes up the me you can't see.

Most of me is made up of dark matter and dark energy.

What are these things, exactly?

That's a secret I'm keeping, for now.

So Much Unseen

Matter is anything that takes up space and has mass. Scientists think there is more to the universe than can be seen. They call this invisible material "dark matter." Based on observations of gravity's effects on visible matter, there is about five times more dark matter in the universe than all the visible matter combined. Of the visible matter, only a small fraction is the bright stuff of stars. The rest is intergalactic gas, which extends outward from galaxies in dimly lit filaments to create a giant cosmic web.

In this artist's rendition, the dark blue areas show where dark matter would have to be to cause the distortion of distant galaxies that astronomers have observed.

All of us—

stars, black holes, you and me, and naughty dogs—

are on the move as the universe expands and we galaxies move apart.

What will happen next?

That's the biggest secret of all.

The Milky Way arches over a
stand of trees in Maine.

What Happens Next?

Astronomers have discovered that the universe is getting bigger faster and faster. What will happen in billions of years? We don't know for sure. Perhaps you will solve the riddle.

Acknowledgments

This edition of *The Secret Galaxy* incorporates 2020 updates from Ashley Balzer Vigil, a science writer for a contractor at NASA's Goddard Space Flight Center in Greenbelt, Maryland. The author and publisher gratefully acknowledge Ms. Vigil's contributions.

Dedications

For the wonderful people at the RPL and at TH. —FH
Dedicated to my parents and my sister, who always encouraged me to chase my dreams; to the International Dark-Sky Association, as they continue to raise public awareness about light pollution; and to the young astronomers among us who will help us learn so much more about our place in the cosmos. —MT

Photo credits

2–3 NASA/Goddard Space Flight Center Scientific Visualization Studio; 6-7 NASA, ESA, and The Hubble Heritage Team (STScI/Aura)/Acknowledgment: P. Knezek (WIYN); 16–17 Wolfgang Brandner (JPL/IPAC), Eva K. Grebel (Univ. Washington), You-Hua Chu (Univ. Illinois Urbana-Champaign), and NASA; 20-21 NASA, ESA, and the Hubble SM4 ERO Team; 24–25 ESA, NASA and Felix Mirabel; 26-27 NASA/JPL-Caltech; 26 (inset) Event Horizon Telescope Collaboration; 28–29 NASA, ESA, M.J. Jee and H. Ford (Johns Hopkins Univ.); all others Mike Taylor

Tilbury House Publishers
Thomaston, Maine
www.tilburyhouse.com

Hardcover ISBN 978-0-88448-391-5
Paperback ISBN 978-0-88448-835-4

Text copyright © 2014, 2020 Fran Hodgkins • Photos copyright © 2014 Mike Taylor unless otherwise noted

Library of Congress Cataloging-in-Publication Data

Hodgkins, Fran, 1964– author.
  The secret galaxy / Fran Hodgkins; photographs by Mike Taylor. —First hardcover edition.
     pages cm
  Summary: "When you gaze into the sky at night, what do you see? Most of us see only the brightest stars because they are the only ones that can cut through the artificial light that overwhelms the night. But up there, beyond the haze of streetlights and buildings, lies the Milky Way--our home galaxy. The words and photos in *The Secret Galaxy* allow young readers to see the stars as never before."—Provided by publisher.

  ISBN 978-0-88448-391-5
  1. Milky Way—Juvenile literature. I. Taylor, Mike (Michael Thomas), 1973- illustrator. II. Title.
  QB857.7.H63 2014
  523.1'13—dc23
                                                            2014014083

Book design by Bumblecat Design & Illustration; jacket design by Ann Casady
Printed in Canada

Fran Hodgkins is the award-winning author of more than 20 books for young readers, including *Hex: The Apprentice* and *How People Learned to Fly*. Visit her website at www.franhodgkins.net. **Mike Taylor** is an astrophotographer whose work has been featured on The Weather Channel, NBC News, Viral Nova, Discovery.com, Yahoo! News, Space.com, Spaceweather.com, Earthsky.org, and NASA's Astronomy Picture of the Day. See his work at http://miketaylorphoto.smugmug.com.